D1442495

SONGWRITING

Scott Witmer

VISIT US AT
WWW.ABDOPUBLISHING.COM

Published by ABDO Publishing Company, 8000 West 78th Street, Suite 310, Edina, MN 55439. Copyright ©2010 by Abdo Consulting Group, Inc. International copyrights reserved in all countries. No part of this book may be reproduced in any form without written permission from the publisher. ABDO & Daughters™ is a trademark and logo of ABDO Publishing Company.

Printed in the United States.

 PRINTED ON RECYCLED PAPER

Editor: John Hamilton
Graphic Design: Sue Hamilton
Cover Design: John Hamilton
Cover Photo: iStockphoto
Interior Photos and Illustrations: AP-pgs 7, 9, 14, 15, 16, 17, 18, & 27; The Beatles/Apple/Parlophone/Capital Records/EMI-pg 27, Corbis-pg 5; David Bowie-RCA Records-pg 12; Elvis Presley/MGM-pg 6; Getty Images-pgs 4, 11, 13, 19, 23, & 28; Iron Maiden-pg 11; iStockphoto-pgs 3, 22, & 24; Jupiterimages-pgs 1, 10, 20, 21, 25, 26, & 29; Katherine Hamilton-pg 31, and 20th Century Fox Film Corporation-pg 8.

Library of Congress Cataloging-in-Publication Data

Witmer, Scott.
  Songwriting / Scott Witmer.
     p. cm. -- (Rock band)
  Includes index.
  ISBN 978-1-60453-696-6
  1. Popular music--Writing and publishing--Juvenile literature. I. Title.
  MT67.W73 2009
  782.42166'13--dc22
                          2009006613

CONTENTS

YOUR FAVORITE SONG

Everyone has a favorite song. Your grandfather may love "Boogie Woogie Bugle Boy" by the Andrews Sisters. A three-year-old girl may sing "Twinkle, Twinkle, Little Star" over and over. Whatever it may be, everyone has a song that gets their blood pumping from the opening note. Maybe it's Robert Plant's scorching vocals on Led Zepplin's "Black Dog." Maybe it's the frantic opening guitar riff of Nirvana's "Smells Like Teen Spirit," followed by the machine gun snare. Maybe it's the simple drums and strutting bass line that opens Michael Jackson's "Billie Jean."

Whatever it is that makes your favorite song recognizable and loved, someone at some time sat down and created it. It sprang from someone's imagination. Perhaps someone's favorite song is sitting in *your* imagination, waiting to be written.

Robert Plant impressed millions of fans with his scorching vocals.

Michael Jackson wrote or co-wrote many of his own songs. The Jackson-penned song "Billie Jean" won him a Grammy Award in 1984.

The *Merriam-Webster's Collegiate Dictionary* defines "song" as: 1) the act or art of singing; 2) poetical composition; and 3) a short musical composition of words and music, or a collection of such compositions. That's a pretty vague definition, isn't it? The beauty of songwriting is that it is limited only by the songwriter's imagination. There are some rough guidelines to songwriting, but the best songs are those that venture "outside the box" and bend the rules.

Most rock songs are "simple" compositions, by musical standards. They most often use three chords, and follow a standard verse-chorus-verse structure. This type of basic form is what makes rock and roll the standard for most "popular music" today. Simple song structure is easier to write, play, and listen to on the radio, as opposed to complex classical music compositions.

In the early years of rock, this basic song structure drew criticism from "serious" musicians. In recent years, however, rock bands have been breaking the mold and experimenting with alternate song structures.

The important thing to remember about rock and roll music is that it has always been about breaking rules. Whether it was Elvis Presley's "provocative" dancing and lyrics, or the punk movement's rejection of authority and conformity, rock music has always pushed boundaries. The songwriting process for rock and roll is no different.

In the early years of rock and roll, Elvis Presley brought a whole new style of music and dancing to the world.

For decades, singer, songwriter, musician, and performer Prince has successfully pushed the boundaries of rock and roll.

INSPIRATION

Before a song can be written, there has to be an inspiration for it, a great idea. Inspiration for songs can be found anywhere: a personal experience, a book, a friend's story, a news article, or even other music. Countless songwriters have written songs about love, which is a universal topic that almost everyone can relate to. Yet, there are millions of other songs that are about other topics, from current events, to politics, to something as everyday as ironing a shirt. It's common practice to tell a story with a song, so your options are limitless. Inspiration for a song can truly come from anywhere.

Many musicians draw on other musical styles, or "influences," when writing music. Singer-songwriter John Fogerty, of Creedence Clearwater Revival, said that Beethoven's "Fifth Symphony" was the inspiration for his hit single "Proud Mary." The band members of My Chemical Romance admit that the early works of Queen heavily influenced their album *The Black Parade*.

In 1975, the band Aerosmith was working on a song. They had the tune, but they were having a difficult time completing the lyrics. Deciding to take a break, the group went to see the movie *Young Frankenstein*. They found Marty Feldman's portrayal of Igor very funny. Inspired, Steven Tyler used one of Feldman's lines from the movie for the title of what became Aerosmith's hit song, "Walk This Way."

Aerosmith found inspiration in a movie theater to complete one of their hit songs.

Girl in a Dirty Shirt

Noel Gallagher of Oasis was inspired by his girlfriend to write the song "Girl in a Dirty Shirt." They were getting ready for an out-of-town gig, and his girlfriend was ironing a dirty shirt because she hadn't brought enough clean clothes with her.

Listening to other music can give you an idea of what you do or don't like about certain songs, and inspire your own song creations. Entire genres of music have been created by musicians fusing two types of music together. For example, the resurgence of "sad folk" music in the mid-2000s is a result of musicians mixing 1960s folk rock with a more modern indie rock sound. Even groundbreaking artists like Elvis Presley and Led Zepplin borrowed heavily from the American blues sound of the early 1900s.

Another common songwriting practice is to borrow ideas from literature. Several rock bands have been inspired by popular or classic books. Metallica's Grammy-nominated song "One" was inspired by the book *Johnny Got His Gun*, by Dalton Trumbo. Iron Maiden composed a 13-minute rock masterpiece about *The Rime of the Ancient Mariner*, a poem by Samuel Taylor Coleridge. In the 1960s and 1970s, many popular artists drew inspiration from current events, including the civil rights movement and the Vietnam War. Rage Against the Machine's music is a great example of politically and socially inspired songwriting.

The Rime of the Ancient Mariner

It is an ancient Mariner,
And he stoppeth one of three.
By thy long grey beard and glittering eye,
Now wherefore stopp'st thou me?...

And I had done an hellish thing,
And it would work 'em woe:
For all averred, I had killed the bird
That made the breeze to blow.
Ah wretch! said they, the bird to slay,
That made the breeze to blow!...

—Samuel Taylor Coleridge

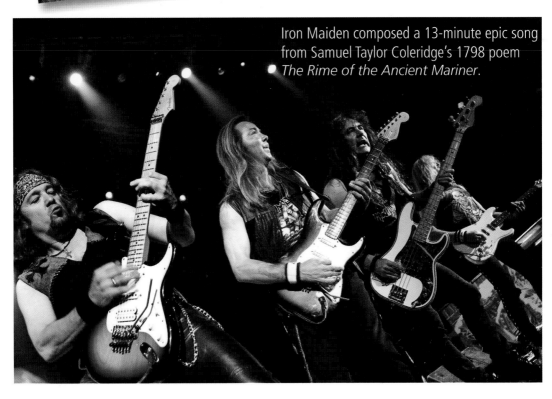

Iron Maiden composed a 13-minute epic song from Samuel Taylor Coleridge's 1798 poem *The Rime of the Ancient Mariner.*

Anything can be an inspiration or an influence on an artist's songwriting. The world around you, the people in it, and the experiences of your life are all interesting places from which to draw lyrics and musical themes.

In 1970, David Bowie was inspired to write a concept album called *The Rise and Fall of Ziggy Stardust and the Spiders From Mars*. Bowie actually played the part of Ziggy Stardust during the writing, recording, and performance of this music. This imaginary character inspired the science fiction and social commentary themes found throughout the album. Bowie wrote his songs as if he was Ziggy Stardust, telling the story of the end of the earth. The album was released in 1972, and remains one of the most important rock and roll albums in history, according to many critics.

David Bowie "became" the character Ziggy Stardust while he was writing, recording, and performing the songs for *The Rise and Fall of Ziggy Stardust and the Spiders From Mars*.

David Bowie performing as Ziggy Stardust.

In the past few years, musical video games have become very popular. Games such as *Guitar Hero* and *Rock Band* have combined the worlds of music and video games. There is much debate whether these games help the music industry or hurt it. Critics warn that these games teach kids that creating music is as easy as hitting a multi-colored button in time with a pre-recorded track. Others say that the games are bringing interactivity to music, and exposing people to music they wouldn't hear otherwise.

Whichever side you're on, it's hard to deny that experiencing music in a new way helps creativity. The games seem to be a good way to interact with music, and learn the underlying patterns that form it. Even if they don't really teach you how to play guitar, the games are an excellent way to learn song structure. They at least introduce people to what it may feel like to actually play an instrument. Perhaps some people will gain the confidence to take the next step, and start their own garage band.

> Musical video games have brought a whole new experience to many people.

> Critics warn that musical video games teach kids that creating music is as easy as hitting a multi-colored button in time with a pre-recorded track. Others say that the games are bringing interactivity to music, and exposing people to music they wouldn't hear otherwise.

LYRICS

There is much debate about lyrics and their importance in rock music. There are people who think lyrics are the most important part of a song. Others see lyrics as secondary to the music. Some rock songs have no lyrics at all. Others have lyrics that mean absolutely nothing. "Baby," by Imperial Teen, is a good example of a pop-rock song with nonsensical lyrics, with such timeless prose as "Who are you I can't recall, I'd rather be at the mall, in a robe and a platinum fall, I'm so thin, I'm so tall."

Many musicians find writing lyrics to be the most frustrating part of songwriting. Others find the lyrics to be the easiest part, and struggle to compose melodies that match the words. As with the other parts of songwriting, there are no set rules when composing lyrics. Some songwriters find it easier to write lyrics after the music has been completed. Others do the opposite, writing the lyrics first.

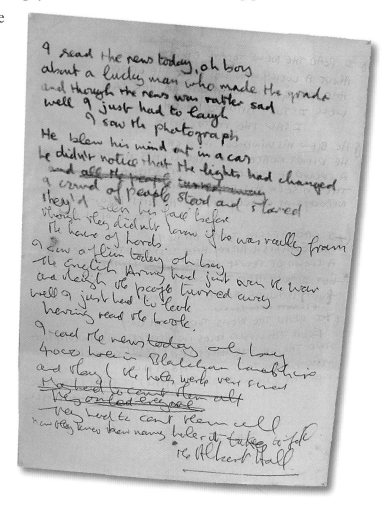

Original lyrics penned by John Lennon for The Beatles' song "A Day in the Life." Some musicians write the lyrics and then the melody, others work the other way around.

KURT COBAIN - NIRVANA

> Nirvana's Kurt Cobain wrote some of his lyrics minutes before recording them in the studio. Other lyricists spend hours or even days working on their lyrics.

Lyrics very often rhyme with the last word of every line, or every other line. Again, there are no rules, and the possibilities for lyrical structure are limitless. Some songwriters at first compose little more than gibberish, and then flesh out lyrics later that make sense. On the other hand, sometimes lyrics flow like magic from a songwriter's mind. Kurt Cobain, of Nirvana, wrote many of his lyrics minutes before recording them in the studio.

Again, there are no concrete guidelines for lyrics in songwriting. Musicians can choose to convey their message either through the music, the spoken words, or both.

SONG STRUCTURE

raditional song structure includes three main parts: verses, a chorus, and a bridge. The verse is normally the "voice" of the song, where the story is told. Verses are usually identical in melody, but feature different lyrics. For example, the first verse could tell about how a boy meets a girl. The second verse could say how the boy loses the girl. In the third verse, the boy could win the girl back, completing the story.

The chorus is "the hook" for the song. It is the main message of the composition. It normally repeats several times in a song. The chorus is usually the part of the song that gets stuck in the listener's head. It is often thought of as the "most important" part of the song, although there is much debate about that. Despite the debate, there is little doubt that choruses are what people most remember about a song. In the summer of 2007, pop radio listeners

were singing the chorus to Rihana's "Umbrella," but hardly anyone knew the words to the verses. The catchy "Under my Umbrella. Ellla. Ella Eh. Eh" lyric was perhaps one of the most infectious choruses in recent memory. Even people who hated the song knew the chorus lyrics. "Umbrella" is a classic example of pop music songwriting.

> Rihana's pop song "Umbrella" is a classic example of pop music songwriting. People easily remembered the chorus lyrics.

Song composers often follow a traditional structure of verses, a chorus, and a bridge. The verse tells a story using different lyrics. The chorus is the main message, and is often repeated. The bridge is the middle of a song.

The bridge is the middle of the song, and is sometimes referred to as "the middle eight," since it is often eight measures long. The bridge is normally where a guitar solo would be featured on a song, or a key change, or something that is a change of pace from the chorus and verses. The bridge normally exists to "break up" a song, and keep it from becoming too monotonous.

As with any type of art, songwriting has no real rules. Musicians freely experiment with song structure, with varied results. Some songwriters do not even use choruses in some songs. Some punk or indie rock songs do not include a distinct bridge. Some alternative rock or art rock musicians do not repeat a verse, but instead have several non-repeating sections of the music that defy any type of verse-chorus identification.

Songwriting has no real rules. Musicians experiment to create their own style of music.

The bridge is normally where a guitar solo would be featured on a song.

MAKING MUSIC

In the past, songwriting was done on sheet music using a centuries-old technique. The notes were written on a "staff," which includes five horizontal lines across the page. The notes were place on, between, under, or over the lines of the staff. Depending on where a note was placed, a musician knew which note to play. Depending on the symbol used to mark the note, the musician knew how long to play each note. Marks at the head of the staff noted the key (or which notes were sharp and flat) and time signature the song was written in.

If this sounds complicated, it's because it is. It can take years of study before learning to accurately read music. However, being able to read and write music on a staff or in musical notation is becoming less of a requirement today for writing songs.

There are several musicians who write great songs, and do not know how to write music in its classic form. The majority of rock bands start out without knowing how to read a single note on a sheet of written music. Robby Krieger of The Doors is a great example of this. He has admitted that when he started playing guitar, he had no idea what he was playing. Krieger played what sounded right. As he continued to make a living as a professional guitar player and musician, he eventually learned music theory and how to write music.

Handwritten Music

> In his early years, Robby Krieger of The Doors played by ear, without music. He played what sounded right. Later, he learned how to read and write music.

The ability to write music is helpful, but not necessary to write great rock songs. There are many rock musicians who write their songs on notebook paper and just note the chords of a song. For instance, the Beastie Boys' "Fight for Your Right" chorus would be noted as A A C D. Writing songs down this way is very easy, and it is easy for the songwriter to communicate to the rest of the band what they are trying to do with the song.

Recently, a form of guitar sheet music has become popular. It is called "tablature." It is an easy way for beginning guitarists to read and write music. In a guitar "tab," there are six lines that represent each of the strings on the guitar. Numbers are written on each string showing which fret to place the fingers, with a "0" meaning that no fingers should be placed on that string. It is very easy to read and to write. Tablature is also helpful for bass guitarists.

Tablature web sites can be found all over the internet with tablature sheet music for nearly every popular rock and roll song ever written. Tablature is a great way for beginning musicians to read music, and learn the structure of songs.

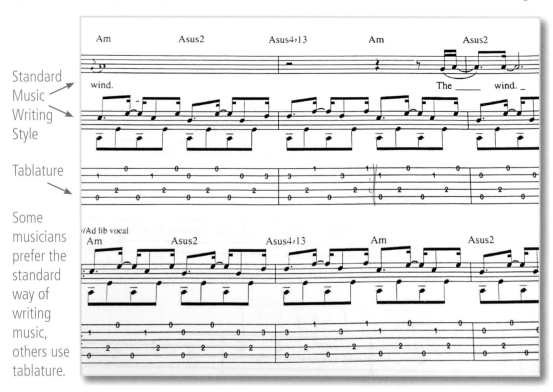

Standard Music Writing Style

Tablature

Some musicians prefer the standard way of writing music, others use tablature.

Musicians compose their music on everything from traditional music paper to notebook paper to tablature.

COLLABORATION

Songwriting is not just a single person's task. Many rock bands compose songs together, or in pairs. This is called "collaborative songwriting." The most famous example of this is Paul McCartney and John Lennon from The Beatles. In the early days of The Beatles, McCartney and Lennon sat down together and composed music, bouncing ideas off of each other and critiquing and improving upon each other's work. This is a method that worked well for them for several years, until their musical ambitions grew in different directions, and they famously split up. Even today, after John Lennon's death, there is an ongoing debate as to whether the songs should be credited to Lennon-McCartney, or McCartney-Lennon. Although their partnership ended badly, the duo produced some of the most memorable and lasting rock and roll songs in history.

Some bands write their songs together.

The songwriting team of Paul McCartney and John Lennon created hit after hit for the Beatles.

Another method of collaborative songwriting is the "jam band" method. This is a technique in which a band goes to rehearsal and just starts playing. The guitar player may have a great idea for a cool guitar riff. He plays the riff, and then the bass player starts to play along, throwing his or her own style into the song. Then, perhaps the drummer picks up a funky beat, something that the guitar player hadn't thought of when writing the riff. Suddenly, the keyboard player plays a jingle that compliments the guitar riff. As it's all coming together, the vocalist starts to sing a melody.

Realistically, the jam band method doesn't usually happen this easily—it's an example of a rare perfect jam session. Still, many bands employ this technique with a great level of success. Some bands even use this technique on stage in front of an audience. They are known as "jam bands," and include such examples as Phish and The Grateful Dead.

Collaborative songwriting with fellow bandmates is popular with many of today's rock bands. Writing with other people can help get those creative juices flowing, even on bad days. It is also a great way to check the quality of your work. If songwriters are honest with each other, they can stop bad ideas before they take up too much time.

When songwriting with other people, it is obviously important to work with someone you trust and respect. Working with other creative people is a great way to make music. The influences of each writer can shine through to produce fantastic results.

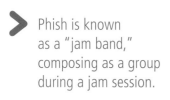 Phish is known as a "jam band," composing as a group during a jam session.

Composing songs during a jam session can be
difficult, but it works for some bands.

GLOSSARY

Bridge

The middle of the song that brings in some kind of change of pace from the chorus and verses. A bridge may be a guitar solo or a key change or anything that keeps a song from becoming too monotonous. A bridge is sometimes referred to as "the middle eight," since it is often eight measures long.

Chorus

The words of a song that are often repeated several times. A chorus is usually the main message of the composition, and is often the most remembered part of a song.

Collaborative Songwriting

When two or more people write music together. Ideas are bounced off of the other person or persons, and then each critiques and helps improve the other's work.

Gig

A job as a musician.

Grammy Award

Yearly awards given out by the National Academy of Recording Arts and Sciences to outstanding artists in various musical categories. The award is named after the gramophone, an early record player.

Lyrics

The words to a song. Some composers create the lyrics and then come up with the melody, while others create the tune and then match the lyrics to the music.

Song Structure

The way a song is composed. Rock songs often have a simple song structure of verses, a chorus, and a bridge. However, songs may be structured in any way the composer chooses.

Tablature

An easy way for guitarists to read and write music. A guitar "tab" has six lines that represent each of the strings on the guitar. Numbers are written on each string showing which fret to place the fingers, with a "0" meaning that no fingers should be placed on that string.

Verses

Words in a song. Often, the words change, but the verses are sung to the same melody.

> Music video games are an excellent way to learn song structure. They at least introduce people to what it may feel like to actually play an instrument. Perhaps some people will gain the confidence to take the next step, and start their own garage band.

INDEX